Little Guides to
Great Lives

LEONARDO DA VINCI

LAURENCE KING

Published in 2018
by Laurence King Publishing Ltd
361–373 City Road
London EC1V 1LR
United Kingdom
Tel: +44 20 7841 6900
E-mail: enquiries@laurenceking.com
www.laurenceking.com

Reprinted 2019 (twice)

Illustrations © 2018 Katja Spitzer

A catalogue record for this book is available
from the British Library

ISBN: 978-1-78627-187-7

Commissioning Editor: Chloë Pursey
Senior Editor: Charlotte Selby
Design concept: Charlotte Bolton
Book design: Stuart Dando

Printed in China

Laurence King Publishing is committed to ethical
and sustainable production. We are proud
participants in The Book Chain Project ®
bookchainproject.com

BOOK
CHAIN
PROJECT

Other *Little Guides to Great Lives*:
Maya Angelou
Marie Curie
Charles Darwin
Amelia Earhart
Anne Frank
Stephen Hawking
Frida Kahlo
Ferdinand Magellan
Nelson Mandela

Little Guides to
Great Lives

LEONARDO
DA VINCI

Written by
Isabel Thomas

Illustrations by
Katja Spitzer

Laurence King Publishing

Who was Leonardo da Vinci?

Artist or <u>engineer</u>? <u>Architect</u> or scientist? Sculptor or inventor?

Leonardo's notebooks – filled with sketches of birds, people, landscapes, flying machines and designs for buildings – show us that he was all of these things.

He was a great artist, but he was also one of the world's first scientists, trying to understand the world by looking carefully at everything around him.

His story began in a village called Anchiano, near the town of Vinci, in the hills of Tuscany, Italy ...

Leonardo was born on 15 April 1452. His parents never lived together or got married, but he was close to both of them. He spent most of his childhood living in his father's farmhouse.

Caterina

MOTHER
Farmer's daughter

Ser Piero

FATHER
Important notary
(an expert in legal
documents)

Leonardo didn't go to school, so there was lots of time for adventure. The hilly Tuscan countryside was perfect for exploring.

One day he wandered into a gloomy cave and discovered the bones of a <u>prehistoric</u> whale, fossilized in the rocky wall.

Young Leonardo was brilliant at mathematics *and* music *and* art. One day Ser Piero asked his son to decorate a wooden shield for a farm worker.

Leonardo thought a shield should be blood-curdling to terrify enemies!

The scariest thing he could think of was <u>Medusa</u>, a gruesome <u>Gorgon</u> from Greek myths. Anyone who gazed at her face was said to turn to stone.

"Perfect!" Leonardo thought, and got to work.

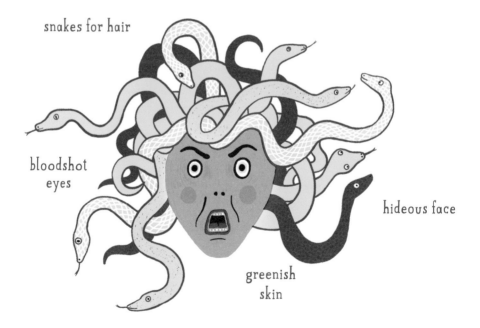

snakes for hair

bloodshot eyes

greenish skin

hideous face

He roamed through the fields and woods, scooping up lizards, crickets, snakes, butterflies, locusts and bats.

Back at home he piled them up to design a disgusting
monster. He painted it slithering from a dark cave,
belching poison, puffing smoke, and shooting fire
from its eyes.

When Ser Piero saw the painting he leapt back in horror. It was terrifying! Leonardo was delighted – his painting had done the job. He realized that art gave him the power to shock people!

Leonardo's father thought the shield was a bit too good for a farm worker, so he sold it instead!

In the 1400s, most sons followed their father into a career. But Italian law said that a child of unmarried parents couldn't become a notary.

Ser Piero hoped that Leonardo could be a professional artist instead. He moved the whole family to the city of Florence, and 15-year-old Leonardo began training with a famous painter called Andrea del Verrocchio.

Ahem! Famous painter, sculptor, goldsmith *and* musician!

ANDREA DEL VERROCCHIO

Verrocchio ran a huge workshop, producing different kinds of art for wealthy customers:

Golden tableware

Decorations for cathedrals

Murals for church walls

Statues for public squares

Suits of armour

Theatre costumes and props

Bespoke stone tombs

What a perfect place for a curious mind!
Leonardo had so much to learn.

Rules of <u>perspective</u>
(which had only just
been invented)

How to work
with clay and
cast in bronze

Grinding colours
and mixing them with
egg yolk to make
permanent paint

The <u>chemistry</u>
of colours

At first, Leonardo worked on small bits of big paintings. Verrocchio's *The Baptism of Christ* was almost two metres tall! Leonardo painted the angel on the left.

THE BAPTISM OF CHRIST

Verrocchio thought the angel was so good, it made his own pictures look mediocre. He put Leonardo in charge of all new paintings and focused on sculpture instead!

After ten years, Leonardo set up his own workshop in Florence. His customers included the Medici, one of the most important and powerful families in Italy.

Leonardo put all of his learning into practice, but he was beginning to rebel against the old-fashioned style of painting.

Instead of dabbing <u>pigments</u> on to wet plaster to create a <u>fresco</u>, he preferred to use oil paints on wooden panels.

Oils dried slowly, allowing artists to paint more slowly and make more changes. Leonardo discovered how to paint silky hair, natural, atmospheric backgrounds, bright, glowing skin and glinting jewels.

GINEVRA DE' BENCI

In busy <u>Renaissance</u> workshops, artists used 'pattern books' to speed up their work. If someone ordered a painting of horses, the artists would copy from a book of horses in different poses.

Leonardo preferred to look closely at nature, and draw what he saw. Even when he drew invented creatures like dragons, he made them look more real by observing real animals.

Leonardo was using art to understand nature better.

19

In 1481, a group of monks asked Leonardo to paint the *Adoration of the Magi*, a famous scene from the nativity.

He started enthusiastically and some think that Leonardo even drew himself into the picture. He was given two years to complete the job, but left Florence for Milan before the painting was finished!

No one knows why Leonardo decided to leave. Perhaps
he was feeling grumpy. The Medici had recommended the
finest artists in Tuscany to decorate the brand new Sistine
Chapel in Rome, but they left Leonardo off the list!

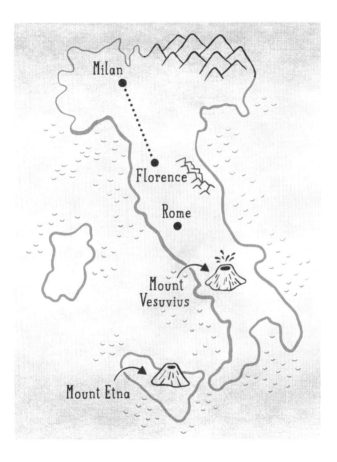

Perhaps he just wanted a change of scene. Milan was
a bigger, richer city than Florence. It was getting
ready for war, and needed engineers.

Leonardo wrote to Ludovico Sforza, the ruler of Milan, describing his ideas for "various and endless means of attack and defence".

I have plans for bridges, very light and strong, that will be indestructible by fire and battle, and plans for burning and destroying those of the enemy.

Where the attack operation fails, I shall make catapults, trebuchets and other engines that will get the job done.

Also, I will make covered cars, safe and strong, which will enter among the enemy.

I have also plans for weapons with which to hurl small stones in the manner of a hail-storm.

In 1482, Leonardo began working for Sforza. He fitted in well with the mathematicians, musicians, artists and scientists who hung around the court. They were the celebrities of the time.

Leonardo spent 17 years in Milan, and his skills were always in demand. Sforza gave him plenty of work, and regular pay.

ENGINEERING

- Casting bronze cannons
- Inspecting army defences
- Inventing weapons
- Designing diving suits and swimming belts

ARCHITECTURE

- Designing domes and towers for cathedrals
- Planning forts, bridges, villas and castles

PAINTING AND SCULPTURE

- Decorating <u>altarpieces</u>
- Painting portraits
- Decorating churches and palaces

ENTERTAINING

- Playing music
- Writing poetry, stories and riddles
- Designing props and costumes for parties and festivals
- Inventing stage machinery

TOWN PLANNING

- Managing water supply and drainage
- Improving health and transport
- Planning locks and canals
- Planning a new city with double-decker streets

Sometimes there was a bit *too* much work, and Leonardo felt frustrated.

He had promised to build a statue of "an enormous horse in bronze, on which rides the Duke Francesco [Sforza's dad] in armour".

Like many of Leonardo's projects, work on the giant horse progressed very slowly. After eight years he began visiting stables to sketch model horses.

How's the horse statue coming on?

What Leonardo really wanted was more time to spend
on his epic search for knowledge.

Leonardo had begun keeping notebooks crammed with ideas – scribbles, sketches, experiments, inventions, memos and shopping lists. He kept adding to them until he died, and together they cover every area of science and the arts.

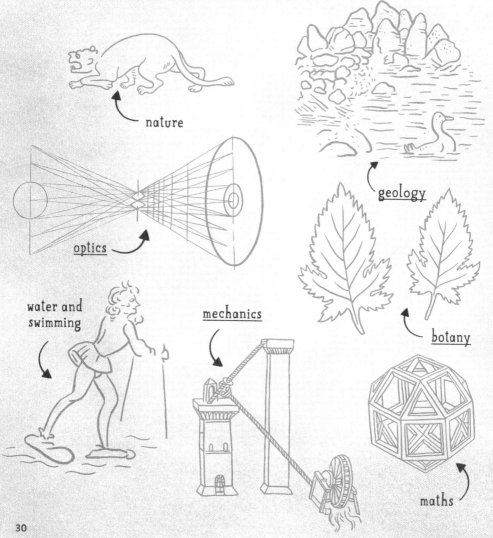

nature

optics

geology

botany

water and swimming

mechanics

maths

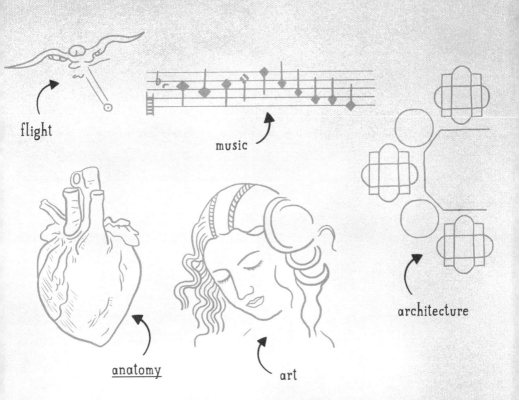

flight

music

architecture

anatomy

art

Leonardo famously used mirror
writing in his notebooks.
Perhaps it was to keep his ideas
secret – he worried that some
of them, like a design for a
submarine, would cause havoc if
they got into the wrong hands!

Rest a mirror here!

One of the things that fascinated Leonardo most was anatomy – the way that our bodies are structured underneath our skin.

Leonardo didn't do much studying from books (at the time, most books were written in Latin, a language he couldn't read).

He learned about living things by drawing them. He wrote down what he saw, and questions that he wanted to answer.

What is sneezing?

What is yawning?

Which muscles raise the nostrils?

Which muscles open and close the pupils
of the eyes?

Why do both eyes move together?

The legs of a frog have great resemblance
to the legs of a man.

Describe the tongue of the woodpecker
and the jaw of the crocodile.

The span of a man's outspread arms is equal to his height

In the 1400s, there were no cameras or photographs. A painting or sculpture was the only way to remember something you had seen. Leonardo wanted his paintings to look as real and natural as possible, and he practised drawing a range of heads.

Drawing helped Leonardo learn about science, and the more he learned, the better his art became.

STUDY OF FIVE GROTESQUE HEADS

But Leonardo was a perfectionist, and was rarely happy with his work.

"Painters often fall into despair ... when they see that their paintings lack the roundness and the liveliness which we find in objects seen in the mirror."

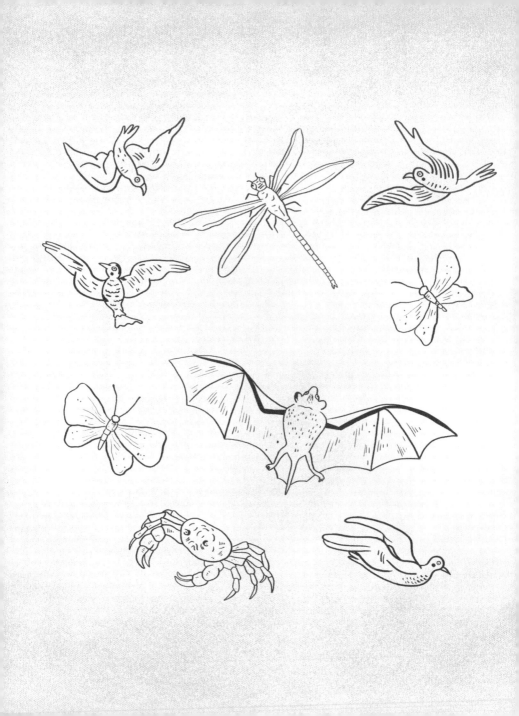

"I wasn't just fascinated by human anatomy. I studied birds and bats and flying insects, trying to work out how they stay up in the air."

Leonardo hoped to imitate nature by designing a machine that could help humans fly. He sketched machines with wings that beat like a bird's.

Just as Leonardo learned about science by drawing, he invented machines by drawing them. He was brilliant at thinking in 3D.

cane skeleton with stretchy leather 'tendons'

pedals pull cables to flap the wings (not just up and down, but inwards too)

pedals pushed with feet

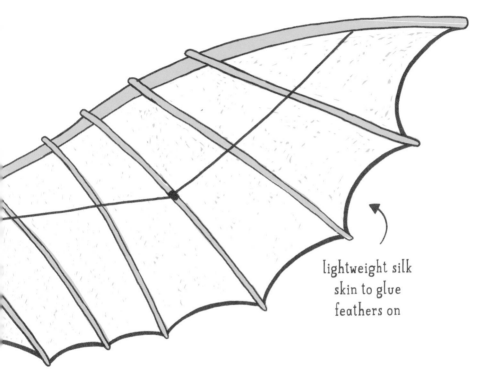

lightweight silk
skin to glue
feathers on

We don't know if Leonardo built and tested
his flying machines – but other people
have! Turn to page 55 to find out whether
one of his designs worked.

In 1495, Sforza asked Leonardo to paint a fresco of *The Last Supper* to decorate a wall in the Monastery of Santa Maria delle Grazie.

A young monk, Matteo Bandello, wrote about watching Leonardo at work:

He would go there early in the morning and climb up on the scaffolding, because the painting is quite high above the ground.

On numerous occasions, and I have seen this with my own eyes, he would not put his brush down from sunrise to dusk, but, forgetting to eat and drink, he would continue to paint.

There were then two, three or even four days in which he did not touch his painting, yet he stood sometimes one or two hours a day just looking at it ...

The monks complained that Leonardo was working too slowly, but he had a good excuse ...

The Last Supper turned out to be one of Leonardo's best ever paintings. It was also the last work he completed for Sforza in Milan.

What about my horse statue?

Like many of Leonardo's projects, the giant horse was never finished. Leonardo got as far as building a life-sized clay model, when French troops captured the city and kicked Sforza out!

Leonardo hastily left for Venice and the model – 7 metres from hoof to mane – was used for target practice.

43

By now, Leonardo was famous all over Italy, and it was easy to find new work. After a brief stay in Venice, he returned to Florence.

The city was at war with nearby Pisa. Leonardo was given the job of redirecting a river to cut off Pisa's access to the sea! It was an impossible task.

He took on new painting jobs too, including an enormous fresco on the wall of the town hall, celebrating Florence's previous victory over Pisa in the Battle of Anghiari.

HOW TO (ALMOST) PAINT A FRESCO

Draw a <u>cartoon</u> to show what it would look like

Build scaffolding in the room

Buy the materials

Prepare the wall with plaster

Transfer the cartoon on to the wall

Pick up your paintbrush

Leonardo was ready to start painting, when disaster struck!

"On the 6th day of June, 1505, Friday, at the stroke of the 13th hour I began to paint in the palace.

At that moment the weather became bad, and the bell tolled, calling the men to assemble.

The cartoon ripped. The water spilled and the vessel containing it broke.

And suddenly the weather became bad, and it rained so much that the waters were great. And the weather was dark as night."

The cartoon was ruined! But as excuses go, it beats 'the dog ate my homework'.

After two years, the Florentine government demanded that Leonardo hurry up and finish *The Battle of Anghiari*, or pay them back.

Luckily Leonardo had friends in high places. The French king, Louis XII, asked that "our dear and well-loved Leonardo da Vinci" come and work for the French governor in Milan.

Leonardo moved back to Milan to work as a court architect, artist and engineer. He took with him another painting he'd begun in Florence but not yet finished – *La Gioconda*, better known as the *Mona Lisa*.

This is one of Leonardo's best and most mysterious paintings. It's special because he managed to show in a painting not just what his model looked like, but what she was thinking and feeling.

LA GIOCONDA

By 1512, Leonardo's French <u>patrons</u> were beginning to lose power in Italy. The following year, Leonardo decided to move to Rome, where the Medici family were now in power.

The Medici put Leonardo up in a luxurious palace, but he didn't enjoy Rome. He shut himself away, studying the structure of the heart, experimenting with lenses and mirrors, and complaining that people didn't take painters seriously enough.

"The painter is lord of all types of people and of all things ..."

Leonardo also amused himself by dressing a lizard to look like a tiny dragon.

Over time, Leonardo grew grumpier and grumpier. When his former patrons King Louis XII and Giuliano de' Medici died, Leonardo despaired. What he was going to do next?

The Medici made me and destroyed me.

In 1515, Leonardo had invented a large mechanical lion – a gift from the Medici to Francis I, the new King of France.

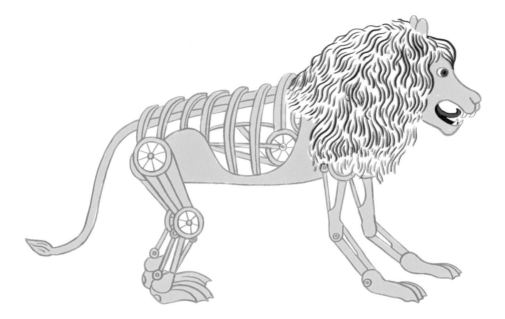

Francis I loved art, and must have been bowled over by the lion. In 1516 he invited 64-year-old Leonardo to leave Italy and become his royal painter.

Leonardo moved to France with his dearest friend, Francesco Melzi. His worries were over. He was paid well, had a big house to call home, and the time and space to paint and study science.

He even got to chat to the King every day.

On 23 April 1519, Leonardo wrote his last ever note – his will. Nine days later he died, aged 67.

As a day well spent brings happy sleep,
so a life well used brings happy death.

Leonardo was well known when he died, but in the last 500 years he has become famous all around the world.

Reading the 7,000 pages of his notebooks is like exploring the mind of a genius. He never stopped asking questions and discovering new things.

As a scientist, some of his ideas and insights were hundreds of years ahead of the rest of the world.

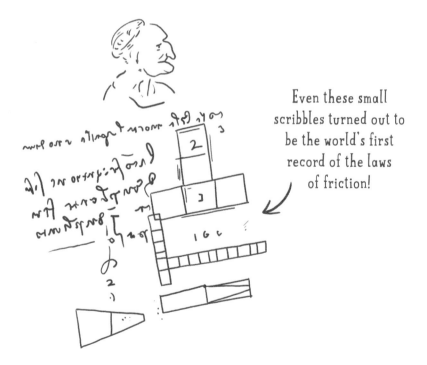

Even these small scribbles turned out to be the world's first record of the laws of friction!

His understanding of <u>physics</u> made him a fantastic engineer, helping him to invent more than 400 machines. He drew the mechanisms in so much detail that they can be built today!

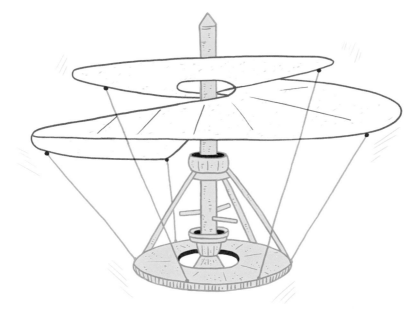

This flying machine didn't work, but it was an amazing idea for the time!

Leonardo's impressive scientific knowledge also helped him to create some of the world's greatest art.

Strangely, for such a famous artist, few of Leonardo's paintings survived – and many that did are not signed or even finished!

It was hard to finish pictures. No matter how long I worked, I always noticed something I wanted to correct.

Luckily, Leonardo liked to keep his sketches and drawings, and these have helped historians to work out which masterpieces he worked on. Around 600 of Leonardo's drawings survive.

He was brilliant at making people and animals look real and rounded. His techniques changed the way that other artists worked.

Leonardo is famous for being a genius. But his notebooks show that, in many ways, he was just like everyone else.

He often grumbled – about people who didn't give him enough respect, people who disturbed his privacy, and work he didn't want to do.

He worried about what people thought of him. And he didn't impress everyone:

"Alas, this man will do nothing,
he starts by thinking of the end of
the work before its beginning."
Pope Leo X

But thinking was what Leonardo was best at. He didn't just want to make things and get paid. He wanted to understand everything that already existed.

He will always be remembered as the world's most curious person.

TIMELINE

1452
Leonardo is born on 15 April, near the town of Vinci in Italy.

1467
Leonardo becomes an apprentice to Andrea del Verrocchio, in Florence.

1473
Leonardo draws a landscape on the *Feast of Santa Maria delle Neve*, his earliest known drawing. He contributes to Verrocchio's *The Baptism of Christ*, which he finishes in 1475.

1482
Leonardo writes to the ruler of Milan, Ludovico Sforza, offering his services. He leaves Florence and moves to Milan.

1483
Leonardo receives a commission to paint the *Virgin of the Rocks*.

1488–90
Leonardo begins working on designs for flying machines including a 'helicopter', a submarine and war machines.

1493
Leonardo builds a clay model of the Sforza horse.

1495
Sforza asks Leonardo to paint a fresco of *The Last Supper* to decorate the Monastery of Santa Maria delle Grazie.

1498
Leonardo completes *The Last Supper* but does not finish the statue of the Sforza horse.

1507
Leonardo is appointed as Louis XII's painter and engineer. He paints a second version of the *Virgin of the Rocks*.

1513
Leonardo moves to Rome and lives in the Vatican, studying the properties of mirrors.

1515
Around this time, Leonardo paints *John the Baptist*. He also constructs a mechanical lion for the new king of France, Francis I.

1478
Leonardo's first commission is recorded, for an altarpiece in a chapel in Florence. His customers include the Medici family.

1479–80
Leonardo is thought to have painted the *Madonna and Child* and *St Jerome*, which he never finished.

1481
Leonardo agrees to paint the *Adoration of the Magi* altarpiece but does not finish the work.

1489
Leonardo begins working on the Sforza horse and embarks on studying human anatomy.

1489–90
Leonardo paints the *Portrait of Cecilia Gallerani* (*The Lady with the Ermine*) and begins his studies on the flight of birds.

1490
Leonardo paints the *Portrait of a Musician*.

1499
The French army conquers Milan, Leonardo leaves.

1500
Leonardo arrives in Florence, and later becomes Cesare Borgia's military engineer.

1503
Leonardo begins *The Battle of Anghiari*. Florence is at war with Pisa. Leonardo begins sketches for *La Gioconda*.

1516
Leonardo leaves Italy for France, where he will serve Francis I.

1519
On 2 May Leonardo dies aged 67.

Leonardo da Vinci

GLOSSARY

altarpiece – a work of art, such as a sculpture or painting, of a religious subject made for placing above and behind the altar in a Christian church.

anatomy – the study of the bodily structure of humans, animals and other living organisms.

architect – a person who plans and designs the construction of buildings.

architecture – the process and product of planning, designing and constructing buildings.

bespoke – made for a particular customer or user.

botany – the study of plant life.

cartoon – a drawing done to prepare for a piece of art. The concept dates back to the Middle Ages.

chemistry – the study of matter (things such as atoms, gases and elements) and how they interact with each other.

commission – an order for something, especially a work of art, to be produced specially.

engineer – a person who designs, constructs and tests structures, materials and systems.

fresco – a painting done on wet plaster on a wall or ceiling, so that the colours absorb into the plaster and become fixed as it dries. This technique was used in Renaissance paintings.

geology – the study, through the examination of rocks and soil, of the earth's structure and how it changes over time.

Gorgon – in Greek mythology the term refers to any of the three sisters (Medusa, Stheno and Euryale), who had hair made of snakes.

mechanics – the working parts of a machine.

Medusa – one of the three Gorgon sisters in Greek mythology. Anyone who looked into Medusa's eyes would be turned to stone.

optics – the scientific study of sight and the behaviour of light.

patron – someone who provides money or other kinds of support to a person or organization.

perspective – the art of representing three-dimensional objects (for example, buildings) on a two-dimensional surface (for example, paper) to give the right impression of their height, width, depth and position in relation to each other.

physics – the study of matter and energy, and how these forces interact.

pigments – a substance used for colouring or painting, which when mixed with oil or water makes paint or ink.

prehistoric – the period of time before written records.

Renaissance – a period in European history, from the fourteenth to the seventeenth century, during which the Western world experienced great change. 'Renaissance' is a French word meaning 'rebirth'.

trebuchet – a machine used in battles to hurl large stones or other missiles (weapons).

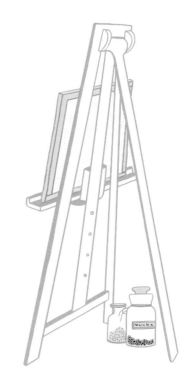

INDEX

CREDITS

Photograph on page 61 courtesy of the Library of Congress